T0353934

THE PURPOSE OF THE CHURCH

To teach you how to live in Heaven
"SUNDAY SCHOOL LESSONS"

ROBERT DENNIS

WESTBOW
PRESS®
A DIVISION OF THOMAS NELSON
& ZONDERVAN

WestBow Press books may be ordered through booksellers or by contacting:

WestBow Press
A Division of Thomas Nelson & Zondervan
· 1663 Liberty Drive
Bloomington, IN 47403
www.westbowpress.com
844-714-3454

ISBN: 979-8-3850-3984-5 (sc)
ISBN: 979-8-3850-3985-2 (e)

Library of Congress Control Number: 2024926130

Print information available on the last page.

WestBow Press rev. date: 12/27/2024

THE PURPOSE OF
THE CHURCH

My opinion for the purpose of the church is it was established to teach you how to live in heaven. Jesus came to earth to Provide a plane form man to be forgiven of his sins so he could be invited to Heaven, He spent three years training His Apostles to teach people how to live and teach them the rules, John 15 vs 16 Jesus told his apostles You did not chose Me, but I chose you. Appointed you that you should go and bear fruit and that your fruit should remain. He also told them when the spirit of truth has come, He will Guide you into all truth. He will not Speak on his own authority. John chapter '1 vs 13. Jesus told Petter after He acknowledge that He was the Son of God. Then He said on this solid rock statement I will build my church And gave him the keys. Matthew. Chapter 16 vs i8 & 19. And The church began on that day of Pentecost Acts 21 The church. The apostles could not take care of everything, that they had To choose some help which they did That story is in Acts chapter The purpose of the church Acts chapter 6 vs 1-7. Men also taught the people. The Church meat on the first day of the week as to recognize the fact that Jesus rose on that day. Thar day is recognized as the Lords Day. The church began to grow in the country and the helpers also went about teaching and many believed Herod, who was king was an enemy of the church. He killed James with the sword. Acts 12 vs 2. He also put Peter in jail. But Herod got his dues, He was at this big event speaking to the crowd. The people wanted to impress him, they kept shouting a long time, then said the voice of a god and not of a man. Then immediately an angel of the Lord struck him because he did not give glory to God. And he was eaten by worms and died. History says he was eaten inside, and it took three days for him to die. Acts chapter 12 vs 21-24 The apostles continue to go about teaching the word to The cities and writing the book for us to live by, one of the rules For us to liv by is in first Corinthians chapter 16 the first four vs, That say on the first day of the week, Let each one of you lay Something aside storing up as he may prosper. This is an obligation If you have prospered, if for some reason you are not there you still have the oblation. The only way you don't is if you did Not prosper. We have many more rules listed in Romans chapter 13 vs 1 and to pay our taxes vs 7 vs 8 owe no one anything but Love vs 9 you shall no commit adultery and you shall not murder And you shall steal and you shall not bear false witness and you Shall not covet and it is summed up by saying you shall love your Neighbor as yourself. We shall not judge our brother chapter 14 vs 10 The church grew so strong and the need for more help Was solved by appointing good men filled with the spirit as Elders They had the responsible to see that the church was run According to the teaching of the apostles. And to take Care of the needs of the church my opinion again the

The purpose of the church was to bring together the people At one place at the same time. To worshiping God together and loving each other being concern for each other, during bigger works, encouraging each other. Being alone is dangerous. Jesus said two are better to walk together. If one falls down the other can help him up.

In the early days of the church the gospel was only for Israel. But later it was extended to the gentiles. There was a good man in Caesarea. But he lacks something, and he was a gentile. He saw a man that told him to send for Peter, and peter came And preached to him and his family and they accepted the gospel And were baptized, Peter had the keys to the kingdom.

Cornelius and his family received the gift of the Holy spirit From that day on the gentiles became members of the church. God wants everyone to be saved. Jesus Told his disciples before he left to go into all the world and preach the gospel to every creature. those that Believe and are baptized will be saved. So, the decision is left to everyone. When the church was one. Now there is over 3000 religions Jesus started the first one It appears the same problem of the past, is that some Have done what they wanted to, remember what Jesus said There are two roads one is narrow the other Is wide, one belongs to SATAN it is more enticing and He will tell you about all the fun you can have on it. But also Remember he wants you and he is a liar and the father of it, and there is no truth in him, John chapter 8 vs 44

THE PLACE

Today we want to discuss the place we want to go To and how to get there and who can we bring with Us. We have been invited to the place where most everyone wants to go to see how to get there and what will it cost. But Jesus is doing the invitation and paid the cost John chapter 14 vs 2 rea in My Father's are many mansions, if it were not so I would have told you. I Go to prepare a place for you. I will come again and receive you unto My self that where I am there you may be also. All you must do is prepare your self. He has left the instruction with his disciples to tell everyone. They wrote them in the book instructed by the Holy spirit, He is willing to share all the goodness and pleasures of his home with us which is the mansions of heaven and rest from the toils Of this life, and from all the troubles that come with It rests from the temple and from the oppression of sin. This will happen when He comes again sharing More than we can imagine. Here are the words from The Holy Spirit. In first Thessalonians chapter 4 vs 16 @ 17 For the Lord Himself will descend from heaven with a Shout, With the voice of an Arch angel and with the Trumpet of God. And the dead in Christ will raise first Then we who are alive and remain shall be caught up Together with them in the clouds to meet the Lord in The air. And then we shall always be with the Lord That's how it will happen some day we just have to be Ready and prepared, the invitation has been sent. Yours Are invited to heaven to be with Jesus and His Father Forever and to be with all the best people that ever Lived. What remains is your decision to be ready, you You don't have to go you decide by the way you live. First Consider what it will cost. We know everything cost Something. Will it be worth the cost. We could be with Our family forever. Jesus has already paid the price with His death. We just must follow His directions to get There. There are obstacles. in our way that we must Overcome. Sometimes it is habits, friends, limitations And sometimes even family. Jesus says in Mathew chapter 10 vs 37 @ 38. He that loves father or mother more than Me is not worthy of me. And that loves son or daughter More than me it is not worthy of me. And he that taketh not His cross and follows me is not worthy of me. Jesus Says going cost you time maybe family and friends. A Cross to bears a burden of hardship persecution from family And friends maybe ridicule and talked about, maybe even Made fun of. But recorded in Revelation chapter 21 vs 7 and 8 is this He that over cometh shall inherit all things and I will Be his God and he shall be my son. But the fearful and Unbelieving and abominable and murders and sexually Immoral, sorcerers, idolaters and all liars shall have them Part in the lake which burns with fire and brimstone Witch is the second death, we will have to over come All the obstacle that stands in the way anything Including a life of sin, they are some of the cost To be invited and accepted life of sin, these are some of the costs to be invited and accepted. could mean more than money, The Second, considering ration is what is in it for me. WE have Arrived seen a mansion home with God. Looked at What is said about that home in Revelation chapter It is a city four square with a wall around it. Made of precious stones. The city was pure gold like clear glass It had a big gate of one big pearl, I have no sun or moon The glory of God and Jesus are the light and there will Be no night vs 27 says in no way will anything that Defiles or causes an abomination or lie will enter it But only those who are written in the Lames book Of life. The benefits will be so good we can't afford to miss them. No police, No sin no need for doctors, No death, no getting old, no infirmity, all will be perfect. After cost and benefits consider the cost between the two.

Jesus gave us this world we just described to come to earth. Was born in a barn, rejected by his own people. That God Loved so much to give up His Son. And Jesus loved the People so much. That as He stud on the hill overlooking Jerusalem that He says oh Jerusalem, Jerusalem Thou Kills the prophets and stones them that are sent unto You. How often would I have gathered thy children together as a hen gathers her chickens under her wings but you would not Mathew chapter 23 vs 23-37 And He prayed to forgive them as they crucified Him. They wanted Him to suffer. Luke chapter 23 vs 34 They did not kill Him. He gave up his life for them And you and me. History says it takes 3-4 days to die from crucifixion, He has provide everything for us. We just must make the choice.

WHERE ARE YOU GOING?

Before you go anywhere, you should find out if the place you are going is where you would like to be. Revelations Chapter 21 gives us a good description of heaven. We will be like the angels in modern day lives. It is out of this world. An earlier lesson was about the place, if you missed, you could find most of the rules to live by in Romans, Chapter 13 and 14.

This lesson is just to get you started. Today we will discuss the question of where you are going. Before you start your trip, you must plan by knowing where you are and knowing where you want to go, we have all demonstrated a certain amount of faith by being here, which is the starting point. First, we must believe the destination is where we want to go. We believe that is the starting point. Our destination is heaven. We must believe that Jesus has invited us to come there. We must now plan how to get there. He has left us a book of instructions. First, we must believe he is The Son of God and confess this. This is the first signpost, so we know where we are. When you are traveling and you know where you have been and now know where you are, you might have a better knowledge of where you are headed, but you must remember there are two roads in life. Jesus said one is narrow, and one is wide. But they don't go to the same place. The wide one belongs to Satan. He will try to get you on the road along with all of his helpers. He will convince you it was easier. You don't have to do anything to get there, but you don't want to be there. There are all types of enticements along that road and remember Satan is a liar, the father of a lie. In first John 8:44 you are still traveling. The next step is to be baptized. This is what Jesus told his disciples ill Mark 16.15-16.

To go all the world and preach the gospel to every creature and that those that believe and are baptized will be saved. Noticed saved comes after baptism. That's when the sins are washed away. And there will be no sins in heaven. Now there is still a long journey to your destination. You will have to stay alert because Satan is detouring your road to his and check your positions in your life at times to be sure you are still on the right road. There is a stop close to the baptism that comes about at the same time and might be moved upon in your travel and that is repentance. This makes a change in your life. Keeps you on the right road. We will finally realize how unworthy we are to be able to be invited to heaven because of the cost that Jesus paid. So, we need to keep our cyes tead on his instructions and remain being of the church which is recorded in Acts 2:38. When Peter said to those on the day of Pentecost repent and be baptized, every one of you and the name of Jesus Christ for the remission of sins and you shall receive the gift of the Holy Spirit. Every day you will be confronted by some obstacles that will try to get you off the narrow road. The church was founded for your benefit so you could come to gather with other people who want to go to the same place as you. You will hear lessons from the teachers to help you get there. You will hear lessons from the preacher to help, and he will be trying to convince others to be a part of your group. And all the people should be encouraging to each other and helping those that need it. Also, refreshing your love for Jesus as a reminder of his crucifixion.

YOUR LOYALTY

We will discuss your loyalty today. Is your loyalty where it is or where it should be? First, we will see what loyalty is. Our dictionary says being faithful to the legal sovereign government. It could be on the national level or state or the local level. Today looks look at the loyal responsibility at the local level.

As we see what loyalty is in I Samuel 26 is the story of Saul trying to find Dave so he might kill him. It is at night when Dave and another person go into Saul's camp. They find Saul asleep. David's partner says the Lord has given him into your hand. Let's strike him with the spear. David said no we can strike the Lord and not be guilty. David would not harm Saul because he was appointed by God. Even that Saul was after him to kill him. Had the situation been reversed Saul would have killed David. David said this the man God had anointed king and I don't have the authority to remove him. The Lord will remove him when the day comes. David shows his loyalty to the one who put him there. Not many months ago I heard much about loyalty conserving loyalty with an oath to a political group. They want the members to be loyal to their party even if it was right or wrong. This is not the kind of loyalty that we are looking for. We have some people who are very loyal to civic or social organizations. They give their time, money and effort in their work. We might ask why so loyal to that organization? They would say I believe what they stand for.

You ask why not some other organization? They would say I don't believe in what they stand for. This kind of loyalty is based on them opinion. This kind is based on what they like and what they want today. Now, where is our loyalty? Is it family? I have heard excuses about families. Say refusing the baptism of family members because them mother or father was not baptized. Sometimes some organizations take our time and money and effort and leave nothing for the cause of Christ. Within our church that earns your loyalty seeing that the preacher is speaking the truth.

Where should our loyalty be? David was loyal to the man God put in this place. Who is over God's people today? Apostle Paul told Titus to set this in order where it was preaching so that the people would know the truth by appointing Elders at every church. Usually means it works like supposed to deserve our loyalty. They have many responsibilities. I will list a few. They are responsible to have a preacher and to see that he preaches the truth. Seeing that they have leaders for each class and to see that lessons are taught. To see that we have a song leader and make sure they have song books. See that the grass is cut and to see after the physical and spiritual needs of those in need. These are just some of the responsibilities that are necessary to worship. Some of these responsibilities are so great that they need to delegate some of the work to others. That office, being ordained by God, demands loyalty and respect for that office so you can find no others over God's people except Elders.

Paul found certain cases with Corinthians that were loyal to preachers and were following preachers. This is condemned. I have heard of certain places where members are loyal to the preacher. Leaving and following them. There is no authority to follow anyone. But elders do we deed in which points remain boil. Do we have the right to decide which points that remain loyal to? We don't have the privilege to choose, which saying of God we can choose which saying of God to obey. There are some who believe they can be saved because of their accomplishments in life and because of who I am. Some learned too late that God means what he says. If You have a group that is loyal and filled with determination you can't find a better group to get things done.

LOSE HIM AND LET HIM GO

In the book of John is a story that is still in existence today. It starts with a group of people walking down the road. They can see a house and as they get closer, they can hear people crying, Martha heard that Jesus was coming so she ran outside to meet him. She said to Jesus if you had been here, my brother would not have died. Jesus said your brother will rise, Martha. She said yes in the last days. Then call her sister Mary telling her Jesus, wants to see her. There was a crowd of close friends of the family, and they all were crying because the brother was dead. Jesus asked where to have they laid him? He was buried in a cave. Jesus was with them, and he also cried for his friend. There was a big rock in front of the cave. Jesus had the people roll the rock away, and Martha said he has been dead for days. He will stink. Then Jesus prayed and said, Lazarus come forth. He did all bound up hands and feet with grave clothes on. Jesus said, "Loose him and let him go."

There are two things to notice in the story. One is the rolling away of the stone. Did Jesus need help to move that stone, or did he want to engage the people? The same thought after he made Lazarus rise from death. Jesus saw a lot of people crying. Jesus had compassion for his own people and cried. Also, he could have done something to the stone, and it would have rolled itself away and the same thing could happen to the grave. Many times, God does what man cannot do. Man has responsibility to some things even for his salvation. We looked at the statement and saw Lazarus was all tied up. Many people are also tied up by many things. Here is an example. Remember Abraham. God told him to leave his family and go to a place he will show you. Abraham had some kin folks with him, and he carried Lot with him. If Lot stayed with him, he had problems. He broke the trust of his family. Family ties can be very tight. You may have heard those who will not obey the Gospel because of family and past say if I do, I will condemn him. That is an excuse because you cannot condemn anyone, nor can you save anyone - only God can do that. Some kindred are opposed to some of their family because some members will look bad by the way he lives. See how some members refused to go to church, some husbands or wives refused to obey because some others refused, too. The bond is sometimes very tight, and they refuse to obey God. Love of riches is one of those ties. It is one of the ties that need losing. Others don't have riches but want to and try to get more. Sometimes it is just greed for the want of money. In Acts 5 is a story of this. A man and his wife want honor from the people because someone else did this. They sold a piece of land and gave all the money to the apostles. Now they used the same plan but to keep some of the money. That is a story of Ananias and his wife who both died because they lied to the Holy Spirit. They had seen other people receiving honor for what they did so they wanted the honor without doing anything to deserve it. One time the Lord told his people you are robbing me. They asked how. He said in the tithes and offerings. Greed is one of the strong ties that bind people of the world and God's people. There is a question of why God's people spend less and less missionaries than the religions. They don't want to part with their money. It is why many good works are not done and why the word of God is not spread through this country by radio and TV. God's people are blessed and keeping the money. What binds modern people today? The unconceived attitude that exists with many. I look after my problems. These problems are not concerns of mine. The world around us influenced but not in favor of God. We indulge in ways of the world. After the lust of the flesh, we are shackled. When we refuse to stand for the rights we are in trouble and do not take lightly something powerful. Hebrews 4:12 says, "The word of God is living and powerful and sharper than any two-edged sword piercing even to the division of soul and spirit." We need to solve what brings us back.

EYES ARE WATCHING YOU

And ears are listening too there are many groups that are seeing what you say And what do you do. They use this information or their advantage and sell it to others. That sounds scary, but that is not the big eye on you, God is hearing every ting you say and seeing everything you do Let's look at some examples. This has been going on for many years.

It goes back as far as Cain and Able in Genesis chapter 4. The story Goes that Cain and Able brought an offering to God. Abeles was approved But Cain's was not. He became angry and as they were walking through The field Cain killed his brother Abel. Later God ask Cain where Able is.

He says I don't know, am I my brother's keeper. God says your brothers Blood cries up to me from the ground. God was aware. Cain is driven out The garden. Now why do you suppose Abel's offer was accepted? Hebrew 11:4 said by faith Abel offered an accepted offering, how do You get faith. Faith comes by hearing says Romans 10:17. It looks like God may have told both what he wanted, and Cain did what He Wanted to.

Just because they don't like you It happen to Daniel Daniel was doing good work for the king. But a group Of men didn't like Daniel. They sought to fine something they Could you accuse Daniel of it? They found nothing, they concede If we find anything it will be concerning the Kingdom. So So, they planned to get the king to sign a law that who Ever prayed to any other God for thirty days would be thrown Into the lion's den. Daniel new about the law, He was in habit of Praying to God three times a day. But that didn't stop him He Went home and prayed as before. These men watched and Found Daniel praying and went and told the king. The king liked Daniel tried to find a way to save him but could not. So They threw Daniel in the lion's den. The king couldn't sleep That night. So, he got up early and went to the lion's den to See what happened. He called out to Daniel, and he answered Saying God closed the mouth of these lions, because I was Innocent before Him and you, so they pulled Daniel out.

And threw the men and their family in that had trick the king You will find this story in Daniel chapter 6 Another story of the watchful eye of God is found about David Whom he loved. But David made a bad mistake and toke Another man's wife. Then had him killed by the army in the war But God sent Nathan to him and told him what he had done and told him what his punishment would be, and it would follow Him the rest of his life, you find this story in 2nd Samuel chapters 11 and 12.

Another story about a man and his wife lying to the Holy Spirit Is Ananias and his wife Sapphira. They sold some land and pretended to claim they gave all the money to the apostles. They wanted the praise of the people. But they agreed to keep some money for them self, and no one would know this. But when Ananias brought the money end to Peter, He asked him why did you lie and keep Park of the money. It was all yours, but you have lied about it and said you not only lied to men but also to God Then he fell dead. Then his wife came 3 hours later, and he told the same story, and she fell down dead. This story is in Acts chapter 5

These stories should convince us that we cannot hide anything from God, In the book of Revelations, God tells John to write to the seven Churches in Asia and tell them of their conditions. They have faults and don't recognize them and that they should do something about it. So, God gives them instructions, then they were all right, But God can see them Many times people do as David did. They do things secretly thinking they are not being seen or go into some place where no one knows them, then they feel save away from their friends theses stores let us know that God is watching and listening to us all the time. The Lord knows our motive for anything we do. Makes no difference what Excuses we might use. If we fail to take part in worship or if we have ill feelings toward a brother or if we get angry and use some excuse and go to some other church. You can't foul God He knows why.

Remember the Lord does not look at the outward appearance of man but at the The rules and laws of God are to protect the innocent and to punish the Off offenders. That seems fair does the thought ever go through your mine recon if God notices s all the good things that I have done. You can be sure That He does. Look at what He says in Matthew chapter 10 vs 42 He says whoever gives one of these little ones a cup of cold water in the name of a disciple will not lose his reward.

We can be sure that God not only sees the evil but also all the Good and even the motive behind them, The Lord also watches over For their good and protection Remember these verses Matthew chapter 12 vs 36 But. I say to you that for every idle word man may speak they will give account of it in the day of judgement this was spoken by Jesus, also spoken by Jesus in Matthew chapter 10 vs 29 He says not two sparrows sold for a copper Coin and not one of them falls to the ground apart from your Fathers Will, Also Isaiah chapter 59 vs 1 says Behold the Lords Hands are not Shorten that it cannot save nor his ear heave that it cannot hear.

WHAT GOD SAYS IS WHAT WE MUST DO

Today's lesson starts in the book of second King's Chapter 5. The Syrians had gone on raids and brought back captives, a young girl from the land of Israel. She became the servant of Naaman, Commander of the Army of Syria. He was a great and honorable man, but he had leprosy. The young girl said to her mistress if only my master were with the prophet who is in Samaria. He would heal him of his leprosy. Then Naaman went and told the king. Then the king said go and I will send a letter to the king of Israel, so he did it and took lots of silver and gold and gifts with him to get him to do what he asked. But the king of Syria was sending him to the wrong person, but he was an important man in that country that he thought the other king was trying to raise a war with him. But the right man Elisha heard about it, and he sent word to the king saying send him to me. So Naaman went with his group to see Elisha. Elisha sent a messenger out to tell him, go wash in the Jordan River seven times and your flesh will be restored to you and you will be clean. And Naaman was insulted and turned away mad but one of his servants said to him if he had told you to do something great wouldn't you have done it? He agreed. Then why not do something simple. He went to the river and did it and was clean. The same argument can be made about God's command baptism. That is a simple act that some people think is foolish and refuse to do it, but it is the command of God and if you don't, you still have your sins, and you won't get into heaven with sins. When God says to do things His way, we will see there is no other way to do it. Look at the story in Genesis. Chapter 4 is the story of two brothers, Cain and Abel. God had told them to bring an offering. Abel's was accepted but Cain's was not, and it made him angry. Why did God approve Abel's? It is stated in Romans 10:17 so then by faith comes by hearing and hearing by the word of God. So, God must have told both of them but Cain did what he wanted to do. Cain was so angry that he killed his brother.

Look again at two brothers who were to bring an offering before God. One did what he was supposed to do, and the other one did what he wanted to do. We will find that when you don't do what God says there is a penalty to follow. This was Cain and Abel. Cain was punished for the rest of his life. Let's look at another example. Two brothers who were priests. They were responsible at the temple. Nadab and Abihu. They handled the censors for the temple. They were in a parade. They had been in the same job for a while, and they had put fire in their censors before. But in the parade, they put on a different fire. They thought God would notice the perfume. The results where the fire came out of the censers and burned them to death. They should have known, but they did it their way. They did not follow God's instructions. There is another prophet that did things his way by the name of Jonah who did not want to do what God told him to do so he tried to run away and hid. So, he got on a boat and tried to hide from God, but you can't hide from God. God told him to go to Nineveh and preached to them. God was merciful with Jonah. He caused Jonah to be swallowed by a big fish. He stayed alive in that fish for three days until he changed his mind and realized he should have gone to Nineveh, so God gave him a second chance. The fish belched him out on dry ground, and he went to Nineveh and preached as God told him to. All the people in Nineveh changed the way they lived. Another man who had no respect for God's way. He was rich and greater. There was a poor sick man laid at the entrance to his property every day. He did not share any of his wealth with this man. He was proud of himself. He says I have everything I need. I will build big barns to hold my wealth and I will just sit back eat and be proud and just be merry. But God said you will die tonight then who will have your riches? He was not convinced about the poor man or God. Now, do you think people today are any different from that rich man? They are not concerned about God. They pay no attention to God's command. Just look around and see how many people are doing something else other than going to church. Where we are demanded to gather to worship God and draw closer to him and to encourage each other. Where are the people that could be here? Maybe they think God doesn't see them. Just read the newspaper and read about things that are more important than being at church or just drive through town and see all the evil places after dark that they will be headed.

WHERE SATAN DWELLS

Many times, man goes thru life thinking or One thing is not that way for years. People Though the earth was flat, and the moon was green cheese Today look at what many think. That hell is the dwelling Place of the devil. Jesus speaks in Matthew chapter 25 vs 41 Saying departs from Me you cursed into everlasting fire Prepared for the devil and his angels. Luke 16 vs 23 records A rich man in hell we have come to believe that the devil is In hell or either safely bound or locked up busily engaged Touching and poking those who we think are there.

I hope more of who the devil is and where he is lets Look at the devil himself and what we know about him, I believe the devil is a spirit and is ever present Everywhere a leader of influence of major forces that not Good or are evil, he is associated with all evil and he is very Powerful or strong. He once was in heaven. He wanted to take Over. There was war in heaven, and he lost and was kicked out So he is out for revenge, you will find this in Revelation 12; 7-9 This shows the devil was strong engaged in battle with angels Of God he thought he could win He fought with angels I believe the devil is a spirit and is ever present Everywhere a leader of influence of major forces that not Good or are evil, he is associated with all evil and he is very Powerful or strong. He once was in heaven. He wanted to take Over. There was war in heaven, and he lost and was kicked out So he is out for revenge, you will find this in Revelation 12; 7-9 This shows the devil was strong engaged in battle with angels Of God he thought he could win He fought with angels That shows how strong he is compared to us. The devil murder and is a liar says John in chapter 8 vs 44 you are of your father the devil the devil Of the lust of your father, he was a murder from the beginning and Not in the truth because there is no truth in him. When he speaks It's a lie. He is speaking of himself for he is the father of lies he is deceitful and smart, being smart he will attack his enemy in there weaknesses. Being deceitful they at many times are unaware Of the attack. Look at how he operates. He has been around since he deceived Eve in the garden of Eden twisted with the truth. A man of God sent on a mission was told not to stay or eat or drink and return a different way, he was decided by an old prophet and lost his life. he will choose the time and place to Attack, After Jesus had fasted 40 days he temped with Food. Satan will make void good works through greed pride or Lust. he will prevent many from being saved, he entered judas Luke 22 vs 3 he enter the heart of Ananias and Sapphira it cost them Their life, Jesus told peter that Satan desired to have him and he Will sift you as wheat Luke 22 vs 31 He also tried Paul who tried to Go to preach Paul says I would have come to you but I was hindered, Paul says put on the whole armor of God that you may stand Against the wiles of the devil. He also recommends Timothy to study to show your self-approved to God to visit the fatherless And widows in their affliction and to keep himself unspotted from the world, another word from Paul says in Hebrews 10 vs 25 forsake not the assembling of our selves together.

THE UGLY DUCKLING

Once upon a time, a hen sat and hatched 15 chickens and one duck, being one-of-a-kind odd, in a lot. Different, others made fun of him. Ridiculed, he tried to act like a chicken, and it made his life miserable.

Now let me tell you about other classes of ugly ducklings. First, Noah was an odd sort. He did not act like his neighbors, did not think, talk, or do like them. God told him to build a boat. People made fun of an old, odd man like Noah, especially when there is no water. They have fun and a good time and enjoyment and living, instead of working. But it turned out different later. Next look at a man named Lot he wanted to go live among wicked people. Because the grass was green, and they had plenty of water and ease of living. But Lot was odd in this place - all around him was different. What do you suppose happens when you are surrounded by odd people? You adapt. Lot was lucky that Abraham interceded for him Next look at Moses a Hebrew among Egyptians in line for the throne of King. He did not act like these at the top. He chose to be different and turned down pleasures, riches, and social standing. Choosing hardship by looking beyond the greater value. He looked at things beyond the present. Next, look at a man named Samson - also odd by appearance. A man from God. He was supposed to be a leader. The Lord told him to stay away from foreign people. That they would lead him astray. Yet Samson flirted with danger. He found a girlfriend with the enemy and Samson did not fit. Next, look at the nation of Israel. God's people. Where God had taken care of. They were different, but they wanted to be like their surrounding nations. They wanted a king. The Lord told them what would happen, that the king would take your sons, your daughters, your money for taxes. But the people insisted they wanted a king.

Next look at the apostle Peter, a faithful follower of Jesus, even to death. While Jesus was being held for a trial, Peter was in the camp of the enemy. He just did not fit. They said you are from Galilee. Yours speech betrays you. We do not know why Peter mingled with that bunch. He did and wound up denying that he ever knew Jesus and when he realized it, it really tore him apart. Let's look at the apostle Paul. He persecuted the church even putting people to death and was on the way to kill some more, but he saw the light and heard the voice. Paul changed his friends. Paul was odd among his old friends and had to leave them.

We may not be that lucky. No one may pull us away from us friends or habits in time before we could lose our life and soul. How many of us would make the same choice as Moses that have fortune and fame offered to you and turn it down? The world today wants pleasure now and our government is helping them just for the tax money. It has legalized online gambling and dope and alcohol all for tax money. None of these things are good for people or not necessary for life.

Men have not changed. They like to be called Christians, while enjoying sin. They like to live dangerously close, climb mountains, shoot rabbits, like to be natural when taking a stand. They like to be on both sides, always on the winning side. Look what happened to Israel. They were warned, but they went ahead anyhow. He also warns us. He says in Matthew 7:13 Broad is the way to destruction and many go there. Straight is the gate and narrow is the way of life if you find it.

Israel acted as a group. We do not have to do that. Salvation is a personal choice but being in the wrong group can sometimes make a difference. We must ask ourselves, are we strong enough to stand alone? This problem has been the downfall of many good, young people feeling everybody is doing it and get with the wrong crowd and be led away.

This is why the church was founded. To get God's people together, to strength each other, and why the disciples went together. If you are out of place like a duck with the chicken, a Christian trying to live in the world you are miserable because you don't fit and should get back where you will belong.

FOLLOWING AFAR

One of the smoothest and sneakiest ways Satan can Separate you from God is to get you to follow him from afar he can convince you many ways to take Away your interest from church. We will look at a few Cases and reasons. The first thing He will convince you is about is you don't have time. Times and People's Habits have changed over the years. Our whole society has changed, I remember years ago all commercial businesses were closed on Sunday. The idea was that everyone could go to church. That was the Lords Day. Then to satisfy the wants of the people. The government started letting them open after 12 o'clock. Then some people had to work. At the places that were open. Being there early.

That toke away their opportunity to attend church. Then more of the best locations saw the opportunity To do more business and started to open on Sunday That trend has never stopped. Now some stores say Their busiest day of the week is Sunday. So, there is No room left in their life for the Lords Day. The thought Of all I work all week I need a day to rest. Sunday is my day off, for others it is their day of fun. For some I Have heard they say the weekend is football days The The invention of television has the attention of many people time. There are also many attractions that are played on Sunday Some local and some that cause you to travel to be there. And there are some more that takes you from the assembly which is a command. Then there are other reasons people don't attend They feel like they don't have that is easy if you don't plan. I have always thought if you were going somewhere and had to ride the bus that would leave at 10 o'clock, and you wanted to go that you would be there when the bus leaves. Some folks use the excuse I just don't feel good and stay home others claim I don' t get anything out of it or don't like the Preacher. There was a national survey that showed two Thirds of the country's people do not attend church four Times a month. Which means we have generations of People that have never taught their children or have taken hey go to church. And those children grow up and The next generation does not know anything else.

Children get most of their learning from one of three Places. First home second from school and third From church. We can see the results of that today.

Since the supreme court took God out of the school. Young people are killing people just for fun, There

There are many excuses that can be used for not attending church

And following a far off. Remember God has left the decision Up to you if you want to come up and live with Him. Let me show you some examples from the Bible. How the Habit takes place. In the book of Mathew, a group of people Came out to take Jesus' prisoner. And all the disciples left Him, One of them wanted to fight. But Jesus rebuked him. They had been with Him for three years and seen all the things, yet they were afraid. Then Jesus said to them. Do You think that I cannot pray to My Father and He Will provide Me with more than 12,000 angles. We can't Image what that many angels could. One destroys all Of the first born of Egypt. This is in Matthew 26.

In Exodus chapter 13 is the story of the nation of Israel. Leaving Egypt. Because all the first born had died Vs 29 tells not only the first born of the people, also of Everything else. We cannot image the Power of God. After all the disciples left Jesus. Peter followed a far of even up to the court House. Peter had promised Jesus a few hours earlier, even if I must die with you I will not deny You. But he did then The Jesus told him Before the roster crows you will deny three times. Then He remember that and went out and cried, From that day Fomr that day on He never did deny Him again but was Always a strong man for Him, the temptation to follow a Far off stacks many people. IT Stacks their conscious and It makes them feel better for the moment. There is another Story that's starts up good and ends up bad. The story of Solomon He was chosen to be King of Israel. And God Blessed him with wisdom and riches. More than any king Before him or after him. Solon had a weakness for women He had 700 wives and 300 concubines. Many of them from A Forigan country. Which God had said not to take a Foreign woman for your wives and do not give your Daughters to foreign men. Solmon Tried to please all these Wives. With their Gods. Which was against God/s command Even with his wisdom He drifted away from God. Some Times even the ones you love can pull you away from Even the ones you love can pull you away from the followingGod. The world is full of people doing things their way.

There are over 3000 different religions in our world today. Jesus said I will build my church. We have been giving the The choice to choose. Because Solomon turned away From God. He planned to take the kingdom away from Him. Solomon had a good servant named Jeroboam Which God used to judge his people after Solomon. He Sent Ahijah the prophet to tell him that he would be the king over ten tribe of Israel when Solomon died. Solomon's Son Rehoboam became king. But he didn't last very Long until the people rebelled and made Jeroboam King over the ten tribes and left Rehoboam with one Jeroboam was afraid that all the people would return to Jerusalem to worship they would return to Rehoboam.

SEPERATION FROM GOD

Isaiah chapter 59 vs. 1 @2 says behold the Lord hand It is not short that it cannot save. But your iniquities have Separated you from God. The prophet Isaiah wrote Concerning the people of his days. You can see from the Statement they were separated. Looking back at the Beginning God created the earth and all that is in it. And saw Tat it was good. Then he made man in his own image. Then Prepared a placc for him. Then he created a helper for him Eve. When the time came, and the population increased The Lord said My Spirit shall not strive with them forever. Then God saw that the wickedness of man was great and that every intent of the thought of his heart was evil. He was sorry that he had made nan But He did fine with one family that was perfect, that was Noah He told him the earth is filled with violence and I will Destroy it. So he told him to build an ark, which he did.

The great flood came and destroyed all the people except Norah and his family. So, God started all over with people He chose His own people and blessed them. The family of Noah which He Blessed and made into a great nation. The nation grew and did Good and bad. Some years they kept his commands other they Disobeyed, so He punished them by giving their enemies Control over them. When they con not stand It any more They would return to God this happen over and over for 100's of years. God chose his owned people and blessed them With all their needs. But they did not appreciate it. They reached the point they did not want God's prophets to lead them. They wanted to be like other nations and have a king. God warned Them of what would happen. They still wanted a king, So God let them Have one, they finally got so far away God came up with a new plan He said I will write my laws on their Heart. And make a new plan And make a new. plan for the world He sent His Only Son To give them a better plan with a promise. This new plan Was to move their hearts back to God. HIS Son was sent to People as a baby and grew up with them. Once grown up. He set out to teach them the new plan, But they still would Not listen. The new plan had a promise that never had Before. It provides away for men to come back to God They were selfish in their own ways.

His Son Jesus spent three years with his disciples teaching And snowing them and the people that He was the Son Of God, giving them away to be his children. The people were arrogant and would not listen They refused him in everything. They hated him so bad they planned to kill Him, He prepared His disciples to carry on the work. Once They recognized who He was, He said I will build my church. On the fact that I am the Son of God The disciples spent The rest of their lives teaching people. Some believed But many did not. And it is still that way. God has provided Away for man to be forgiven for his sins. But he must make The decision for himself. He must live by the rules that God has given him. First Is how to become a forgiven person Witch Jesus gave to his disciples when He went back to Heaven to be with His Father. Which is written in Mark chapter 16 vs 15 @ 16 which say to them go into all the world and preach the gospel to every creature, He who believes and is baptized will be saved, but who does not believe will be condemned, that makes him a child of God, now he must live by the rules. And he will have Satan and the whole world to be his enemy. He should have all the children of God to be His friends and encourage him God, s plan was to have the first day of the week as a place to gather and worship God and remember Jesus And to encourage each other, and to pass your offering.

At that time, you would be taught the rules He wants you to live By There are so many things that cause people to separate Themselves from God. I have seen many divine visions take Place with families over small decisions such as two people Marring. Both went to two different churches. And could Not agree where they would grow now. Sometimes they Each would go to different ones. Sometime one of them just quit going and I've seen faithful families come all their life then when their children get grown, they don't go at all. My guess is too much other things take their time.

IS IT I

Begin reading Matthew 26:2. Did you ever wonder at the close of service when a person has come forward and says I have not been faithful and wondered astray? I know you are not answering other people's deeds. I also realize many exciting things that seek to pull one from service of God, but did it ever occur to you could have been the one that pushed him just a little? Do you ever wonder how many went astray that never came back? How would I stand and view Matthew if that is because of my actions someone went astray and never returned. With this in mind let's see if I can make some possible reasons that could cause someone to go astray. First, let us take the possibility of going against better judgment. Remember, Adam and Eve. Adam did fall because of someone close he trusted. You and I could be playing the part of one to a weaker member in church. By doing something for us by going to places and committing acts that will do harm to us. But through the eye of a weak brother, it could be that gentle push that sends him on the wrong road.

Remember what Paul said if my brother is offended at my eating meat then I will not eat meat. Wouldn't it be wonderful if we all had this attitude? Since we mentioned this word attitude, let's talk about our attitude for a moment. I believe we can do more to offend with attitude than any other way I know. We have, at times, small insignificant decisions to be made that at times all the possible solutions are all right; yet, here are two ways to go, either are all right. When the attitude of some is that we will do it my way or else I will have no part in it. What would make to our salvation if we had services at 9:30 or 10:00? What if we sing two songs or three songs? What if we have individual communion cups or two large ones? I have heard of congregations falling apart because of such. I have seen members leave the congregation because he did not like the preacher. Let us ask is this the attitude becoming of Christians? Is this type of influence good for the cause of Christ? Is this the kind of light that we need to let shine to bring glory to the name of God?

What kind of influence does this have on a weak brother? Just sitting over to the side taking no active part. He could say if this is brotherly love then I want no part of it. What about our attitude toward our responsibilities and duties as Christians? What kind of influence do we send out when we stay home from services? It is very easy to get into the habit of staying home. If you recall, the Parable of the Talents were each given a different amount but was expected to do all he could with what he had. Well, we have done that. They are our responsibilities to be fulfilled. Let's look at one more example in the Parable of the Samaritan. How at first a priest came by and saw a man wounded laying there in need of help, but he had the attitude of I haven't got time. Let someone else help him. Next came Levite. Both men of God took the same attitude of let someone else look after him. Today there are many in the church with the same attitude Could our actions be that we set an example before that they believe. I was led to believe that all I had to do was attend occasionally and give a little of my means. Later, I thought that since I was doing so little, and it was all right that even a little less would be acceptable, so I quit. We should ask ourselves what kind of attitude we have and what kind of light do I project to others.

RESEARCH FOR SURE TO KNOW

Before Jesus was sent to the earth. God had his own favored people
There were other people on the earth. They all did what they wanted
Do. Even His people didn't follow His rules many times. Neither had
a Promise from God. He used their enemies to punish them at times
They did not appreciate all that He was doing for them.

Jesus was sent to bring in a new law for all the people to show God's
Love to all people and give them promise of coming to live In HIS
house. If they followed all the rules and did what He asked They are to
do. And not the things He did not want them to. Jesus I did not intend
to stay here forever. He selected 12 apostles to teach the The world of
what they should do and instruct others through the church To teach
others. The apostles said before the last one died that the Known world
had heard the teaching. There were some people in All the time that
wanted to be the top one. And to do everything His way. They have
even started their own church, we have over Three thousand religions
on the earth beside the one Jesus said He would Build. And there are
some that want to run the countries their way to That is something
I don't understand. I would think that rulers would They want their
country to be the best they could make it. And they could Help each
other by trading things from one another the other doesn't Have. But
that has not happened down through history. And guess It never will.
The churches' purpose is to teach people how they should Everyone

loses in a war Learn to live in Gods house when they get there. If they don't, they I want to get invited. Jesus said He was coming back to get them. And take them up to live in his father's house with him. But only if you A QUALIFY we now have lots of people to teach, but we have something Early people did not have. We have written instructions. We can read All the rules we should follow are on how people should live and How to treat each other. Loving is better than hating each other or trying To take advance of each other. But some people want to be the king,

The bible book of Romans gives us lots of rules to live by in chapters 13 N 14 And things we should not do. And even to be subject to the Governing authorities. In romans chapter 13 and 14 it says Love does no harm to a neighbor therefore this is the full Full filament of the law Genesis 9 vs 6 says whoever sheds mans Blood by man his blood shall be shed, For in the image of God we He made man snice we are created in the image of God, We should Live to show respect to God by the things we do and say Proverbs Chapter 6 list six thigs that God hates None of these things should.

We are guilty of it. Our government has given us lots of liberties of things that we can do, that are not good for us to do or for other people. Many of them are harmful even to us, just because something is permitted Does not mean we do it. There is a lot of people being killed in our Country and being blamed on guns, guns are only a tool. People are to blame, every law of every level of government has laws that say not to kill God is the giver of life and He alone is the one with authority to take it or delate it to government This book was written to encourage more people to read the bible where all the instructions are.

Printed in the United States
by Baker & Taylor Publisher Services